The Si

The Sixties

Photographs by the
Daily Mail

Maureen Hill

This is a Parragon Book
First published in 2003

Parragon
Queen Street House
4 Queen Street
Bath, BA1 1HE, UK

Text © Parragon
All photographs © Associated Newspapers Archive

Produced by Atlantic Publishing

A catalogue record for this book is available from the British Library.
ISBN 0 75259 026 X

Printed in China

The Sixties

The "baby boomers" came of age in the swinging sixties. Mary Whitehouse tutted as the Permissive Society got into its stride. Lady Chatterley and the Pill went on sale, hemlines rose, hippies said: "make love not war". The Beatles and Stones fought it out in the charts; Mods and Rockers did the same at seaside towns. Pop fans strained their ears to pick up Radio Luxembourg and Caroline, then Tony Blackburn hit the airwaves to launch Radio One.

Twiggy and Jean Shrimpton had the look every woman wanted; curves were out.

The hovercraft and Concorde made their debuts, while Neil Armstrong made "one giant leap for mankind". The Mini was the last word in urban chic, although drivers now had to beware the breathalyser.

Spurs became the first team of the century to achieve the Double. Celtic and Manchester United lifted European Cup. Ramsey's "wingless wonders" were crowned world champions. Muhammad Ali floated like a butterfly and stung like a bee - but the bell saved him against "Our 'Enery".

Some things arrived, and stayed. We went to comprehensive schools; we found things to buy in Yellow Pages, and paid for them with credit cards; "Florizel Street" went into production, expecting a short run. At the last minute its name was changed to Coronation Street. From the momentous and the apocalyptic to the offbeat and the trivial, the photographs in this book, from the archives of the Daily Mail, chart the people, places and events that made up a memorable decade.

The Sixties

Teenage idol

On the sixteenth of September 1960 Donald Campbell was to push Bluebird to over 300 mph before crashing on his second run at an incredible 365 mph, sustaining a fractured skull and various minor injuries. The car however was destroyed and subsequently shipped to Australia for rebuilding, where, at Lake Eyre some four years later, an undeterred Campbell would pilot Bluebird to a new record of 403.1 mph.

Opposite: By the end of the 1950s the power of rock 'n' roll to inspire rebellion amongst the youth had diminished considerably and the rock 'n' roll sound had been diluted and assimilated into the mainstream. In 1960, against this background, pop stars such as Adam Faith and Cliff Richard projected themselves as responsible and clean-living. Opposite, teenage singer Adam Faith poses for a portrait by society photographer Archie Parker. A hit with the youth of the day, Adam Faith was remarkably successful, at nineteen earning £600 a week.

De Gaulle meets Macmillan

President Charles de Gaulle of France inspects the guard of honour on his arrival in Britain for talks
with PM Harold Macmillan. De Gaulle was credited with keeping Britain out of the European
Economic Community (EEC) or Common Market since its inception in 1957, prompting Britain to
devise the rival European Free Trade Association (EFTA) in 1959. By 1961 Britain was attempting to
persuade the EEC to allow EFTA to join the Common Market, but de Gaulle vetoed this.
Opposite: Stirling Moss (centre) ended a frustrating Formula One season in 1960 with a win in the
United States. Graham Hill (right) ended his disappointing year with yet another retirement. He
finished only one race all season in his BRM.

Spurs at the double

Tottenham Hotspur and Northern Ireland football captain Danny Blanchflower was happy enough to be celebrated on the football pitch, here holding the FA Cup aloft after winning the 1961 final against Leicester City to win the league and cup 'double'. However, he was to capture the public interest when he refused to appear on *This is Your Life*. He found it difficult to explain his reasons for refusing to participate in what was one of the most popular programmes in 1961.

Jimmy Hill and the maximum wage

Jimmy Hill turns out for Fulham FC. In 1961 Hill was the chairman of the Professional Footballers' Association (players' union) and led negotiations that abolished the maximum wage for footballers in June, allowing the top players to earn a fortune for their talents. Injury put paid to any chance of a long career and instead Jimmy Hill went on to become the face of football on television throughout the Seventies and Eighties.

Opposite: The legendary Stanley Matthews warms up before the match in which his team, Stoke City, beat Chelsea. Matthews returned to Stoke in 1961, towards the end of a phenomenal career which he had begun there as a schoolboy. By 1965, aged fifty, Matthews was the oldest player in the football league, and in thirty-three years had never been booked. That year he would also become the first footballer to be knighted.

Rod Laver's Grand Slam

Australian Rod Laver holds the Wimbledon Men's Singles Cup in July 1961. Laver was probably the best male tennis player of the 1960s and was the only player to win the Grand Slam twice; first as an amateur in 1962 and again as a professional in 1969. He won Wimbledon four times, in 1961 and 1962, before turning professional and being banned, returning to win the first two open championships in 1968 and 1969.

Opposite: President John F. Kennedy and Prime Minister Harold Macmillan pose for the cameras at a break during talks in Bermuda where they met to consider world affairs, including civil unrest in the Congo, as well as the continuing Cold War.

Khrushchev meets Kennedy

Above: Historic first meeting – Soviet Prime Minister Nikita Khrushchev meets President John F. Kennedy at the American ambassador's residence in Vienna in June 1961. In October of the following year the two were to be major players in the Cuban Missile Crisis which brought the world to the brink of nuclear war.

Opposite: Princess Grace of Monaco at the swimming pool on Monaco beach, four years after her fairytale marriage to Prince Rainier.

Iron mum

Margaret Thatcher's first ministerial appointment came in 1961 when she became a parliamentary secretary to the Ministry of Pensions and National Insurance. She is pictured reading her eight-year-old twins Carol and Mark a bedtime story.

Opposite: Although the initial rebellion of rock 'n' roll was fading in the 1960s, the impact that teenagers had made set the stage for a focus on youth that would gain momentum throughout the decade. When President Kennedy was elected in 1960 at the age of forty-three, he became the youngest-ever elected US president, and with his glamorous wife, and courting of artists and musicians, Kennedy appeared to embody the promise of a belief in youthful idealism and optimism.

Light entertainment

Television became hugely popular during the 1960s, and whilst there were continual concerns over the quality of its output, particularly in regard to commercial television companies, the public generally embraced the proliferation of light entertainment. Host of *Take Your Pick*, Michael Miles, with Mrs Emily Ayerst who tried unsuccessfully to win a Trip of a Lifetime on the popular quiz show. Viewers were so touched by her desire to see her son in Australia that their donations and P&O's gift of a free return sea passage enabled her to make the trip.

Opposite: Peppi and Jackie Roast demonstrate the new dance – the Twist. The Twist craze was started by Chubby Checker as a typical pop gimmick and was quickly embraced by young and old alike, as easy and fun to do.

Dancehalls

An integral part of liberated and hedonistic youth was the way in which young people chose to express themselves through fashionable dress, make-up, hairstyles and the music they listened to. Teenagers and twenty-somethings had more money and leisure time than ever before, and the desire to spend both time and money enjoying themselves socially. A scene from a dancehall in 1961. *Opposite*: A twist on the Twist – the Apple Twist. Sidney and Colin Wilmot demonstrate the dance which involves keeping an apple between foreheads as you dance the Twist.

Twisting the day away

The Twist crossed all generation divides; here a group of schoolchildren perform the dance in the street.

Opposite: Let's twist again like we did last summer. Watched by some suspicious French citizens a pair of British youngsters take part in a twisting competition on the dock at Calais in June 1962. They had crossed the channel on the *Royal Daffodil*, spent three hours twisting in France and then returned to Britain.

Fitted kitchens

Above: Wrighton fitted kitchen units in simulated teak with pale grey marble effect plastic work tops teamed with crimson, saffron and sapphire paisley pattern wallpaper and blind are the height of fashion in this display from the 1962 Ideal Home Exhibition.

Opposite: The Gas Pavilion at the 1962 Ideal Home Exhibition shows all the latest gas appliances, including a built-in oven and counter hotplate. The kitchen's colour scheme is sunshine yellow and white.

Bachelor Boy

The Queen shakes hands with Cliff Richard in the foyer at the London Palladium after the Royal Command Performance on October 29 1962. Cliff would soon be back at the top of the charts for three weeks with 'Bachelor Boy'. To his left is Rosemary Clooney and to his right, Harry Secombe and Eartha Kitt.

Opposite: Wilfred Brambell (left) and Harry H Corbett pose with Hercules the horse in advance of a new comedy series, *Steptoe and Son*, which would run from 1962 to 1974. Harold Steptoe was played by Harry H Corbett who had been born in Burma, before being raised by his aunt in Manchester. He had served with the Royal Marines during the Second World War, and was a member of Joan Littlewood's Theatre Workshop at Stratford, East London in the 1950s.

The beehive

Opposite: Fashionable hairdresser Vidal Sassoon of Bond Street puts the finishing touches to the hair of singer Miss Denney Dayviss. The 'beehive' hairdo was very popular during the Sixties, achieved by backcombing the hair until it resembles candy floss and then smoothing the top strands over.

Above: A group of stylish girls enjoy a dance, seemingly unencumbered by their hairstyles, and afforded greater freedom of movement by ever-shortening hem lines!

Faces of the Sixties

The proliferation of images of young, 'beautiful people' heralded new definitions of social status based on fashion and lifestyle, led by designers, pop and film stars, artists, models and the like. Amongst the most famous faces of the Swinging Sixties was model Jean Shrimpton, the 'Shrimp', a favourite of the photographer David Bailey.

Opposite: Sophia Loren, born Sofia Scicolone in Rome in 1934, became a leading Italian actress during the 1950s and by 1960 had been taken up by Hollywood. She starred in *El Cid*, and with Peter Sellers in *The Millionairess* in 1960, and won an Oscar for her performance in *Two Women* in 1962.

Carry on Sid

Opposite: Sid James, with his wife Valerie, helps promote Koo tinned peaches on a stand at the 1963 Ideal Home Exhibition. A South African by birth, Sid James made his name as a comic on British radio and TV, in shows such as *Hancock's Half Hour* before going on to star in the *Carry On* films. *Above*: One of the first sub-cultural groups to emerge in the early 1960s with a definitive style were the Mods, who like the Teddy Boys of the Fifties took particular pride in their appearance. Unlike the Teds however, whose fashions harked back to Edwardian modes of dress, the Mods were consciously and overtly up to date, wearing the latest tailored suits, listening to modern jazz and American R&B. Here a group of smartly dressed lads queue to enter a nightclub.

Thank Your Lucky Stars

Opposite top: A line up of some of the stars of ITV's autumn schedule for 1963, including (left) Patrick Macnee and Honor Blackman from *The Avengers* and Brian Matthew (centre) from *Thank Your Lucky Stars*.

Above: Sixteen-year-old Marlene Gibson dances 'the Mod' with Gary Davis at the Savoy Ballroom, Ipswich. She is credited with inventing the dance.

Opposite bottom: This group of youngsters, attending a dance at Stratford Town Hall, seem to exhibit elements of both Mod and rock 'n' roll fashions; note the leather jacket and quiffed hairstyles of the two boys at the back. It would not be long however before Mods and Rockers would delineate themselves as two very distinct and opposing groups.

The Greatest

Opposite: In 1960, boxer Cassius Clay had won the gold medal as a light-heavyweight at the Rome Olympics, and was rapidly gaining attention for both his virtuoso talents inside the ring, and the eloquent, though sometimes arrogant way in which he handled himself verbally outside of the arena. In June 1963, Clay was to defeat Henry Cooper by a knockout, in the fifth round of their fight in London.

Above: Any time, anywhere: students on a Florida beach do the Twist.

The rise of Margaret Thatcher

Above: Conservative candidate Mrs Margaret Thatcher talks with Mrs Grace Simmonds during a canvassing tour of the Finchley constituency during the 1964 general election. The Conservatives were to lose this election and all the subsequent elections during the Sixties but by the end of the decade Mrs Thatcher was the Shadow Minister for Education.

Opposite: Freddie, of Freddie and the Dreamers (right), poses with *Daily Mail* competition winners at the Ideal Home Exhibition, John Smiles and Miss Lily Noble. Freddie and the Dreamers, who had started out in skiffle groups in the north of England, had a number five hit in November 1964 with 'I Understand'.

I have a dream

Above: Martin Luther King during a visit to London. The black civil rights leader was a prominent and eloquent speaker and had suffered arrests for leading peaceful civil rights marches in the southern United States. He was assassinated in Memphis, Tennessee in 1968 soon after urging his followers not to abandon the path of non-violent protest.

Opposite: 1964 was the year that Beatlemania swept across the world and the Beatles took both the British and US charts by storm, yet despite the massive explosion of British musical talent that this encouraged, it was only the Rolling Stones who could challenge the Beatles' headline-grabbing abilities. The Stones infused pop music with a new creativity and rebelliousness fostered by their art school sensibilities, presenting a more 'dangerous' and aggressive image than most of their contemporaries.

(l-r: Charlie Watts, Keith Richard, Mick Jagger, Bill Wyman and Brian Jones)

Welcome to the street

Granada Television launched the gritty, northern soap opera *Coronation Street* across the ITV
network in May of 1960, and despite the prevalence of kitchen-sink drama at the time, no one could
have predicted that the series would still be running, let alone attracting regular audiences in excess
of ten million some forty-three years later.

Above: Doris Speed and Arthur Leslie as Annie and Jack Walker give a publican's welcome to fans on
the set of *Coronation Street*.

Opposite: Bernard Youens and Jean Alexander join *Coronation Street* in June 1964 to play what was
to become one of the show's favourite couples – Stan and Hilda Ogden.

Home Style

Opposite: Mr Pastry, actor Richard Hearne, a children's television favourite, fishes for charity donations in the ornamental fountain at the Ideal Home Exhibition.
Above: Pop singer Dusty Springfield who had hits in the 1960s with 'I Only Want to be With You' and 'You Don't Have to Say You Love Me', checks out the latest in home fashion in 1964.

The Pink Panther

Peter Sellers and Britt Ekland married in February 1964, the same year that Sellers was to first play Inspector Clouseau in *The Pink Panther*. It was also the year in which Sellers suffered a heart attack. Here he recuperates with his wife by the pool of their Beverly Hills home.

Opposite: John Alderton and his first wife Jill Browne examine a refrigerator, quite a luxury item in 1964. Both were stars of popular television series *Emergency Ward Ten*, appearing as Dr Richard Moore, and Nurse (then Sister) Carole Young, respectively. Alderton was later to marry the actress Pauline Collins.

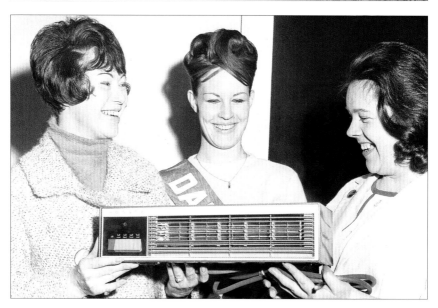

Sixties Songbirds

Above: Three singers, (left to right) Kathy Kirby, Cilla Black and America's Brenda Lee, take a break from rehearsals for 1964's Royal Variety Show.

Opposite top: Bruce Forsyth entertains the singers the Beverley Sisters (left to right) Babs, Joy, Teddy who were his guests at his cabaret show at the Talk of the Town. It was the twins Babs and Teddy's 32nd birthday and Joy's 34th.

Opposite: Lifestyle choices were not merely restricted to high street fashions and hairdos in 1964, as consumer culture became more deeply rooted. In the domestic sphere there was a constantly growing range of innovative electrical goods aimed at families and housewives, such as this portable electric heater.

That Was The Week That Was

Though Conservatism remained entrenched in many areas of society, growing importance was
afforded to the ideas of the younger generation as the beginnings of a dramatic shift in wider social
attitudes, represented in part by an increase in satirical comedy which made fun of Establishment
values. *That Was The Week That Was*, a satirical television programme hosted by David Frost (opposite), included singer Millicent Martin (above) amongst its team.

Pussy Galore

Sean Connery was to play Ian Fleming's literary creation, secret agent James Bond, in the first Bond film, *Dr. No*, and continued to appear as 007 on several occasions up until 1983. Here he meets Honor Blackman who played the leather-clad, crime-fighting Cathy Gale in the TV series *The Avengers*, and who was to star opposite him as Pussy Galore in 1964's *Goldfinger*.

Opposite: Honor Blackman receives the news that she is to play Bond's girlfriend Pussy Galore.

Mods ride into town

Above: Whilst the term Mod had originally applied to a small group of well dressed existentialist London 'jazz types', by 1964 the name was being applied to a wider group of trendy youths, a sub-culture who favoured scooters, pork-pie hats and parkas, and sometimes indulged in amphetamines and violence.

Opposite: Patrons of Hammersmith Palais demonstrate the Zizzle, a new dance.

The Beatles take a break

Above: After a hectic time for the Beatles, including their first US performances and a UK tour, the Fab Four all holiday separately in advance of their first world tour. John and Cynthia Lennon arrive at Luton Airport having enjoyed a well-earned break.

Opposite: Premier Harold Wilson at a Labour Party rally in the Albert Hall with Lord Clement Attlee, the last Labour Prime Minister before Wilson.

General Election '66

Above: Harold Wilson inspects posters in the Press Room of Transport House, the Labour Party's HQ, in preparation for the election in October 1964. Labour were to win the election with a tiny majority of five seats. Wilson successfully gambled on a second election in March 1966 and was given a 98-seat majority and a clear mandate to govern.

Opposite: Dr Richard Beeching, Chairman of British Railways, relaxes in a mock-up of a new design for a first-class lounge on high-speed trains expected to be introduced by 1966. Ironically, he was to be remembered for axing hundreds of rail services across Britain.

Shout

Above: Lulu – the little girl with the big voice. Lulu was typical of girls, like Cilla Black and Sandy Shaw, from working-class backgrounds for whom talent was a passport to success in the sixties.
Opposite left: Most serious television presenters, and all newsreaders, were male. Joan Bakewell managed to break into this male-dominated world.
Opposite right: Joanna Lumley, typical of the Sixties dollybird, played the role with aplomb in several TV series; here dressed in classic early Sixties plastic mini-dress and white plastic boots.

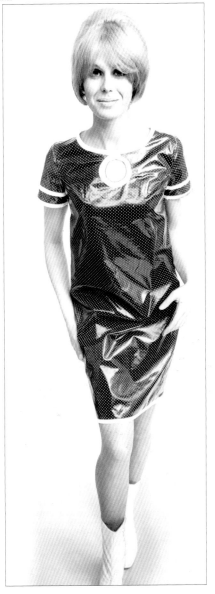

Inner city life

Children play on a wooden climbing frame against a backdrop of concrete, towered over by high-rise blocks of flats. The high-rise was widely introduced in an attempt to deal with the housing crisis that had existed before, and was exacerbated by WWII. There remained a great deal of sub-standard housing marked for slum clearance, homes damaged during the war, and a need for new housing in the wake of immigration, internal migration and the 1960's baby boom. Tower blocks were thought to offer a fast and efficient solution, being easy and inexpensive to erect, and utilising minimal land and labour. Towards the end of the decade however, various design faults became apparent, tragically highlighted by the disaster at Ronan Point in 1968, when an explosion caused the collapse of several storeys, encouraging a change in government housing policy.

Opposite: Easter 1965, and Mods on Brighton beach are watched over by police. Previous Easter Bank Holidays had seen vandalism and violence in Clacton and Margate as Mods clashed with Rockers or 'Greasers' who rode powerful motorcycles, wore black leather, and were a throwback to biker gangs represented in such films as 'The Wild One' of the 1950s.

Death of Winston Churchill

Above: The funeral of Sir Winston Churchill: a huge public occasion in which the nation mourned the death of the leader who did so much to save the country from Nazism.

Opposite: Prime Minister Harold Wilson shakes hands on parting with Ian Smith, Premier of Rhodesia who was in London for talks to try to avert the move to black majority rule in his country. Smith failed to get agreement and one month later, in November 1965, announced a Unilateral Declaration of Independence which was to last until 1980 when the colony finally gained true independence with majority rule, changing its name from Rhodesia, named after colonist Cecil Rhodes, to Zimbabwe, the name of an ancient African city.

The Fifth Beatle

Opposite: England were not only to host the football World Cup in the summer of 1966, but were to triumph in the final against West Germany at Wembley Stadium. Gordon Banks, England goalkeeper throughout the tournament, keeps the ball out of the net in training.

Above: Young Manchester United star George Best in full flow. Best was to prove for many one of the greatest footballers of all time, but in this developing age of celebrity cultural icons, Best, sometimes nicknamed 'the fifth Beatle', was equally well known for his other passions; womanising and drinking.

World Cup winners

Opposite: Jimmy Greaves, injured during the earlier rounds, puts his arm around an exhausted Alan Ball, who had played his heart out during the World Cup Final against West Germany. The match went to extra time, England eventually winning 4-2.

Above: Bobby Moore, surrounded by his team, gives the Jules Rimet trophy a kiss.

Heroes

Above: Three of England's World Cup winning heroes and West Ham team-mates: (left to right) Geoff Hurst, who scored a hat trick in the final against West Germany, Bobby Moore, captain, and Martin Peters.

Opposite: In 1964, Cassius Clay, who was to adopt the name Muhammad Ali, had beaten Sonny Liston to win the World Heavyweight title. Here he weighs in for his second fight with Britain's Henry Cooper.

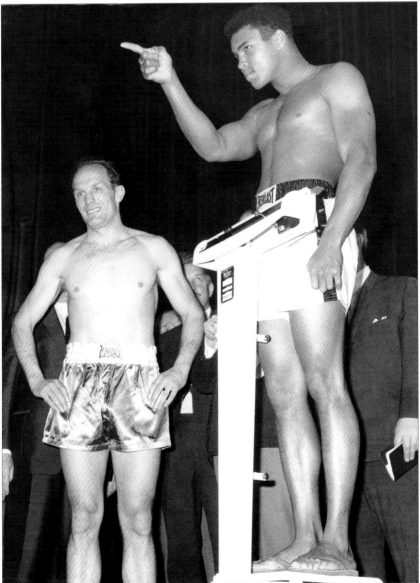

Concorde in the making

Opposite: A prototype of Concorde, the world's first and finest supersonic airliner. Concorde made its maiden flight in 1969 and looked then like something decades ahead of its time. Here, Prince Philip gets a preview at the planning stages.

Above: Mary Quant had set the ball rolling in 1963 with her new, youthful style but by 1966 Carnaby Street had become the centre of the fashion revolution. It was also an essential part of the itinerary of a tour of swinging London.

Matchstickmen

Above: The painter, L. S. Lowry photographed in his living room with some of his paintings. Lowry only became widely known as an artist quite late in his life, and in 1966 the Arts Council mounted a travelling retrospective exhibition of his work starting in Sunderland, moving to Manchester, Bristol and finally the Tate, London.

Opposite: Twenty-year-old Sonia Ross is crowned Miss Britain 1966. Pictured with her are runners up Nanette Slack (left) and Maureen Lidgard-Brown.

'Till Death Us Do Part'

Above: (left to right) Anthony Booth, as son-in-law Mike, Una Stubbs as daughter Rita, Dandy Nichols as Else and Warren Mitchell as Alf Garnett rehearse the edition of *Till Death Us Do Part* to be broadcast for Christmas 1966. Despite the increasingly liberal views of the time, and although satirical, it was perhaps telling that the programme caused more offence due to Alf Garnett's coarse language than because of the character's explicitly racist views. Campaigns for racial equality raged throughout the 1960s, particularly in the US, led by Martin Luther King and Malcolm X, and though Britain passed its first Race Relations Act in 1965, which would help to shift public opinion, penalties for discrimination were minor.

Opposite top: A demonstration of a new dance, the Bend, invented by pop group Dave Dee, Dozy, Beaky, Mick and Tich.

Opposite bottom: Miss Britain 1966, Sonia Ross, models the latest fashion wigs at Birmingham's Ideal Home Exhibition.

Street games

Above: Girls play in the street a recently introduced game - 'elastics' or American skipping. Traditional forms of rope skipping, ball games, hide and seek and chase remained popular.
Opposite: The deckchair dress designed by Anne Tyrell uses the bold stripes and colours of classic seaside deckchair fabric.

Jagger and Richard charged with possession

Gallery owner Robert Fraser, and Keith Richard and Mick Jagger of the Rolling Stones, were charged with possession of cannabis and some amphetamines at Keith's Sussex home in February of 1967. Robert Fraser was found in possession of heroin.

Jagger and Richard were found guilty of drug offences at Chichester court, and given custodial sentences. They were bailed the following day, pending an appeal, which eventually cleared them. Fraser was given a six-month sentence of which he served four months.

Above: Richard leaves his home on the way to Chichester court.

Hey, hey we're the Monkees

Above: Perhaps the first of the manufactured pop bands, the Monkees proved a hit with teenage girls the world over. The band's songs were almost incidental to their TV programme which was a mix of sitcom, music and offbeat humour.

Opposite: Marlene McFadyen, Miss Scotland 1967, poses for the camera with Miss Wales, Dawn Sullivan.

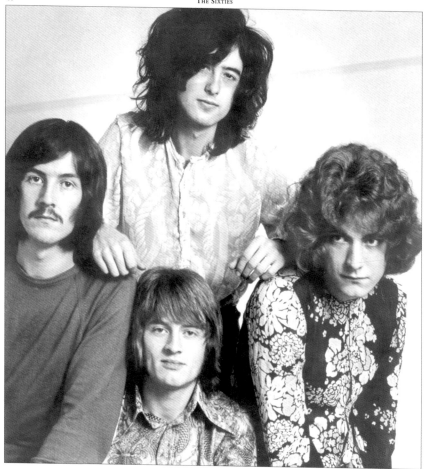

Heavy Rock

London's music scene flourished in the mid-to-late Sixties as psychedelia took hold. Jimi Hendrix moved to London in late '66, and underground bands such as Pink Floyd and Soft Machine produced the soundtrack to the hippie counter-culture. Led Zeppelin were at the heavy end of the rock spectrum and their albums sold well.

Opposite: Mick Jagger's girlfriend Marianne Faithfull was another familiar face on the London music scene and was present at the drugs raid at Keith Richard's home. It was widely reported at the time that she was found wearing only a rug.

Best Boutique

Above: Arch-rivals on the pitch, George Best and Manchester City's Mike Summerbee were close friends off it. The two fashion-conscious stars joined forces to open their own boutique, Edwardia, in October 1967.

Opposite: While there were numerous models and dollybirds around in the Sixties, the face and the body of the Sixties have to be those of the teenage Lesley Hornby, known to the world as Twiggy.

The Avenger

Above: Avenger meets Author. Diana Rigg, Emma Peel in *The Avengers* meets David Frost at a Foyle's Literary Luncheon. Frost, well known from *That Was The Week That Was* and the *Frost Report* was guest of honour, with Antony Jay, as they launched their book T*o England With Love.*
Opposite top: Arsenal centre forward, George Graham, marries model, Marie Zia, at Marylebone Registry Office. Terry Venables (left) is best man, who despite playing for rivals Tottenham is a good friend of the groom.
Opposite bottom: Elsie Tanner, played by Pat Phoenix, marries her American boyfriend, Steve, played by Paul Maxwell in an episode which was viewed in nearly nine million homes.

Sgt. Pepper

1967 saw the release of the Beatles' groundbreaking psychedelic album *Sgt. Pepper's Lonely Hearts Club Band*, and Paul McCartney's admission to having used LSD. The Beatles were also amongst the signatories of a petition in *The Times* calling for the legalisation of marijuana. In June the Beatles were to perform the specially composed 'All You Need Is Love' on the first global satellite TV link-up, their last live televised performance.

Opposite: Joan Collins was raised in a show business family and began performing at a young age. By the 1950s she had appeared in various Hollywood movies and although she continued to do so throughout the Sixties, appearing in *Warning Shot* in 1967, Collins directed most of her attention at this time to her family; her husband, actor and singer-songwriter Anthony Newley, and their two children.

Flower Power

The US government had supported South Vietnam since 1954 as a bastion against Communism, and in the early sixties was maintaining a military presence in the form of 'advisors', as guerrilla warfare raged, funded by the North Vietnamese. However, following a military coup in the South, and the assassination of President Kennedy in the US, the situation was to become even more volatile. In 1964 President Johnson pushed a resolution through Congress enabling him to begin a massive air and land offensive in Vietnam in 1965. By 1967 however, following the ravaging of the country by immense bombing and napalm campaigns, and the evacuation of some thirteen million people from rural areas with very little military progress, the war was becoming increasingly unpopular both in the US and abroad, giving rise to a massive international peace movement.
Above: The anti-war movement was represented by many different factions; there was a peaceful element comprised of hippies and other alternative groups whose direct actions consisted of sometimes absurdist Happenings and street theatre, such as placing flowers in soldiers' gun barrels at demonstrations, but there were also some radical left-wing factions condoning and encouraging anti-social and criminal behaviour in order to disrupt the war effort and resist the perceived wider social evils of capitalism.

The 60s' disc jockeys

Opposite top: BBC's team of disc jockeys and announcers: back row (left to right) Tony Blackburn, Jimmy Young, Kenny Everett, Duncan Johnson, Robin Scott (programme controller), David Rider, Dave Cash, Pete Brady, David Symonds; middle row (left to right) Bob Holness, Terry Wogan, Barry Aldiss, Mike Lennox, Keith Skues, Chris Denning, Johnny Moran, Pete Myers; front row (left to right) Pete Murray, Ed Stuart, Pete Drummond, Mike Raven, Mike Ahern, John Peel.

Opposite bottom: The MG sports car was the car to be seen in, unless of course, you had one of the new Minis!

Above: Minister of Transport, Barbara Castle, takes a spin with rally driver Paddy Hopkirk to test out the safety belts in the Mini-Cooper rally car. The previous year, 1967, she had introduced the breathalyser in an attempt to cut the death rate from drink driving.

The TV shows

Above: Lew Grade was one of the most successful television producers of the 1960s, commissioning programmes such as *Sunday Night at the London Palladium, The Saint, The Prisoner, Emergency Ward Ten, Crossroads, Thunderbirds* and *The Muppets*, and producing the *Pink Panther* films. In 1967 he was given the Queen's Award to Industry, a first for the entertainment business, and in 1969 was knighted for his services to British exports.

Opposite: Winner of the 1968 Eurovision Song Contest, Mary Hopkin, who sang, 'Those Were the Days', a song based on a Russian folk melody and produced by Paul McCartney at Apple Records.

Tony Blackburn launches Radio One

Opposite top: Top Radio One disc jockey Tony Blackburn, who launched Radio One the previous year, playing The Move's 'Flowers in the Rain', poses with Anita Harris and her dog, Albert, during the launch party for a new ITV show *New Release* which he was to compere.

Above: Dennis Tanner to marry and leave mum, Elsie, all alone. Philip Lowrie who plays Dennis Tanner in *Coronation Street* will leave the series after eight years' service. Elsie Tanner, played by Pat Phoenix, has proved to be one of the biggest draws for viewers to the programme.

Opposite bottom: (left to right) Peter Purves, Valerie Singleton and John Noakes, presenters of BBC's *Blue Peter*, hold a litter of Labrador puppies, one of whom will be selected to be trained as a Guide Dog, following in the footsteps of Honey, the first *Blue Peter* Guide Dog.

Ideal living

Above: Home fashion on display at the 1968 Ideal Home Exhibition. The Opus 22 pictured here starts at £18 10s for a basic unit.

Opposite: The Queen is shown one of the latest model gas cookers at the Exhibition's Diamond Jubilee.

Swinging Sixties

A young woman, presumably wearing a mini-skirt and bearing a bag from the Ideal Home Exhibition, pushes a pram decorated with the Union Flag, or Union Jack. The flag was incorporated into all sorts of designs in the latter half of the Sixties as Britain became synonymous with cutting-edge fashion and style.

Opposite: Radio One DJ Tony Blackburn, with a smile almost as wide as his collar. Blackburn remained at Radio One until 1984 when he moved to a commercial station, Capital Radio.

Royal family gathering

Above: A family gathering in 1968 for the Queen's 42nd birthday in the gardens at Frogmore, Windsor. Charles, aged 19, Anne 17, Andrew 8 and Edward 4.

Opposite above: Clean lines and simple geometric designs are the key features of home furnishings in 1968, and a mainstay of female fashion throughout the decade.

Opposite below: Despite some fairly extreme experiments with clothing, taking advantage of new materials and some risqué styles, towards the end of the Sixties, there was something of a backlash against the most revealing and perhaps popular, garments, the mini-skirt and hot pants, and some skirt lengths headed back towards the knee. In the case of the maxi, which also became popular around this time, it was thought that even a skirt that covered the ankles could maintain sex appeal, leaving, as it did, more to the imagination.

United triumph in Europe

Opposite: Manchester United were to win the 1968 European Cup Final against Portuguese side Benfica, with the invaluable help of George Best. The teams were level at one goal apiece as they entered extra time, but Best scored within two minutes of returning to the field, and Manchester United eventually won 4 – 1.

Above: George Harrison with a group of Hare Krishna followers. The Beatles had all become interested in and influenced by eastern, and particularly Indian, mysticism, but George seemed to feel more drawn to the teachings of the Maharishi Yogi than the others. He also learned to play the sitar, an Indian instrument like the guitar.

Fashion capital of the world

Opposite: Yves Saint Laurent with Betty Catroux (left) and Louise de la Falaise outside his New Bond Street premises. As London became the fashion capital of the world it attracted designers from more classic fashion centres.

Above: Singer Clodagh Rodgers wearing her trademark hot pants which were all the rage in the late sixties. Rodgers began singing aged thirteen and went on to feature in various musical films and performances. In the late Sixties she was to have some solo success, and represented Britain at the Eurovision Song Contest in 1971 before moving into country music.

Bobby Kennedy assassinated

Opposite bottom: Entertainer Sammy Davis Junior signs the book of condolence following the assassination of Robert Kennedy after making a victory speech in Los Angeles on 6 June 1968. Robert Kennedy had been doing well in the primaries and was tipped to be the second Kennedy President, following on from brother John, assassinated in November 1963.

John and Yoko

John Lennon and Yoko Ono visit the parents of James Hanratty, hanged for murder in 1962, as they plan to make a film proving his innocence. Inconsistencies in the case were to play a part in the abolition of the death penalty.

Opposite: President Richard Nixon, who had unsuccessfully campaigned for the US presidency in 1960, came to power in the US in January1969. Here he is seen with Prime Minister Harold Wilson at 10 Downing Street in February 1969 during a presidential tour of Europe.

Heath leads the Tories

Above: Edward Heath acknowledges the applause at the Conservative Party Conference in October 1969. Heath became the first elected leader of the Conservative Party in 1965, and would become Prime Minister in 1970. In the final year of the Sixties the Labour Government continued with its liberalising agenda by lowering the voting age to eighteen, easing the divorce laws and confirming the abolition of capital punishment.

Opposite: President Richard Nixon makes an unscheduled stop to shake hands with Londoners outside Buckingham Palace. He had been having lunch with the Queen during his European tour.

Queen opens Victoria Line

Opposite: The new Victoria Line was officially opened by the Queen in March 1969. The journey was the first a reigning monarch had ever made by Underground. The line stretched from Victoria to Walthamstow and was the first in-town Underground to be built for more than sixty years. New features included closed-circuit television, automatic trains and fare collection.
Above: A young Jeffrey Archer canvassing for support for the Conservatives.

First man on the moon

Opposite: In 1961, inaugurating the Apollo space programme, President Kennedy promised that man would set foot on the moon by the end of the decade, and whilst he would not live long enough to see it, on the twenty-first of July 1969 Neil Armstrong would descend the ladder of the Lunar Module, before a live television audience of about 600 million viewers, and set foot on the moon. However, whilst the Apollo 11 mission could be seen as a technological milestone, a victory over Russia and certainly as spectacular television, the point of putting a man on the moon was lost on many of those actually involved in the mission.

Above: A fan dances in the aisle at a Rolling Stones concert at the Saville Theatre in December 1969. In July, two days after the death of guitarist Brian Jones, the band had played a free concert in Hyde Park.

Changing fashion

Above: As the Sixties come to a close youth fashion begins to find a harder edge in reaction to flowerpower and hippies. Skinheads crop their hair and wear more austere clothing.
Opposite left: The maxi – a response to the short skirts which were the fashion throughout most of the Sixties. Here, student Linda Redfern wears a long, dusty pink jersey coat from Bus Stop with a matching furry felt hat from Biba; huge orange sunglasses and an Indian fabric bag complete the outfit.

Last dance at the Locarno

Above: Twenty-five-year-old Tony Jacklin celebrates after winning the 1969 British Open Golf Championship, the first Briton to win for 18 years.

Opposite: End of the Sixties and the end of the Locarno Dance Hall, its neon sign flashing for the last dance.

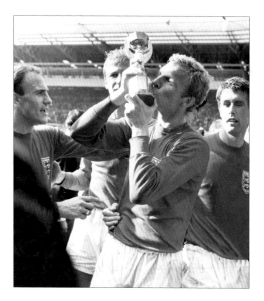

ACKNOWLEDGEMENTS

The photographs in this book are from the archives of the *Daily Mail*.
Particular thanks to Steve Torrington, Dave Sheppard, Brian Jackson, Alan Pinnock,
Richard Jones and all the staff.

Thanks also to Cliff Salter, Richard Betts, Gareth Thomas
Peter Wright, Trevor Bunting and Simon Taylor.
Design by John Dunne.